FASHION FENG SHUI FOR MEN

Bring Fulfillment and Prosperity to Every Aspect of Your Life

GERALDINE WIJSBEEK, FFIPI, FFSM, WYEF

FASHION
FENG SHUI

Copyright © 2018 by Fashion Feng Shui International, LLC. All rights reserved.
13 Wheeling Avenue, Woburn, MA 01801, United States of America
www.fashionfengshui.com

We support copyright. Thank you for buying an authorized edition of this book and for complying with copyright laws by not reproducing, scanning or distributing any part of it in any form without permission.

First Edition: January 2018
Printed in the United States

Fashion Feng Shui is a registered trademark and the stylized "F" logo and the phrases "Work Your Element", "Transform Your Look and Life", "Dress for Your Dreams" and "Create Closet Harmony, Live Your Best Life" are trademarks of Fashion Feng Shui International, LLC.

This book is available at special quantity discounts for bulk purchase for sales promotions, premiums, fundraising and educational needs. For details, write to sales@fashionfengshui.com.

Edited by Karina T. Hof [http://karinahof.com/]
Art direction by Rebecca Wijsbeek [http://www.rebeccawijsbeek.nl/]
Cover design by Alex [https://www.fiverr.com/alerrandre]
Layout by Too Fabulous For Words [http://toofabulousforwords.com/]

Table of Contents

Introduction 1
Our Outlook 3
Transformational Triad 5
What Fashion Feng Shui® Can Do for You 7
When You Might Need Fashion Feng Shui® 9
The Five Elements 11
Water: The Philosopher 13
Wood: The Pioneer 15
Fire: The Pleasure Seeker 17
Earth: The Peacemaker 19
Metal: The Perfectionist 21
Identify Your Essence 23
Your Authentic Self 29
Physical Appearance 31
Essential Dressing 35
Case Studies 39
Transform Yourself through Fashion Feng Shui® 53
Dress Your Intention 57
Conclusion 61
About the Author 63
About Fashion Feng Shui® 65

Introduction

No matter how old you are, discovering who you really are at your very core is a wake-up call. Once you come to see and understand it, many things will suddenly reveal themselves. You'll be more confident. You'll have more direction in life. You'll create better and more meaningful relationships. Our lives have many twists and turns, and nothing ever stays the same. If you're already living the life you always envisioned, may you continue to stay true to that vision. If you haven't yet achieved the dreams you had for yourself, whether as a child, as a young man, or as an ever-evolving adult, *Fashion Feng Shui for Men* can help as you set out to achieve those dreams and, in so doing, discover your inner essence—the real you.

Fashion Feng Shui for Men teaches men of all ages how to implement changes in their wardrobe to get more love, find more empathy, achieve more success and gain more attention—for all the right reasons. This, in turn, leads to creating better life-flow, which leads to improving your quality of life. When you dress with intention, your clothes express your authentic self. That helps you achieve your desires, from those that are buried deep within to the most external, such as weight loss.

"Feng Shui" means "wind-water." It is the ancient Chinese art of placement, based on a system of honoring energy, known as "Qi." Nature is in perfect harmony and the elements of Water, Wood, Fire, Earth and Metal interact in perfect balance. Fashion Feng Shui® is a person-focused style system that was designed using the five elements theory integral to Feng Shui. This unique approach to clothing and accessorizing allows us to dress—and address—all aspects of ourselves: mind, body and spirit. The application of Fashion Feng Shui® helps you create just the right symmetry in your life to attract perfect Qi (chi).

Our Outlook

Fashion Feng Shui® is a person-focused style system that was created by Evana Maggiore. It applies the ancient Chinese art of placement to harmonize to our most intimate environment, our closet. As a transformational styling technique, Fashion Feng Shui® teaches us how to choose clothing that flatters our appearance, functions for our particular lifestyle, fulfills our essence and fortifies our intention. Whether in work, or play, or at rest, harmonizing our inner and outer worlds, through what we choose to wear, helps us be our most authentic selves.

Fashion, style and upkeep of personal appearance have long been seen as the focus of females. But today, it's becoming more apparent that males have similar interests and concerns about how they look, how they present themselves to the world and how others perceive them.

In the same way Fashion Feng Shui® has advised women all over the world, this approach to dressing also encourages men to identify their essence, understand their physiognomy and dress in a way that respects both. Fashion Feng Shui® guides men on a path to getting well-groomed and well-dressed, regardless of lifestyle or budget. That, in turn, helps them feel comfortable in their own skin, make a good first impression and gain respect in both their professional and their personal lives. According to the basic principles of Feng Shui, everything in the universe is comprised of five elements.

Nature's five elements bring balance to your wardrobe
Your personal Qi (chi) is connected to everything in your immediate surroundings, be it in your private or professional life. Feng Shui enables us to create balance and harmony in our home or office, but applying Fashion Feng Shui® increases both your internal wellbeing and your external successes. Its foundation is the creation of harmony through yin and yang—the balance of everything, which helps you stay happy and content.

FASHION FENG SHUI FOR MEN

Color is an important component of Feng Shui. Different colors are used to represent each of the five elements: Water, Wood, Fire, Earth and Metal. Color therefore plays a leading role in dressing with intention (what we most desire in our lives). This can be a long-term goal or something you require just for today. Our daily moods are affected by colors: bright, vibrant hues may lift us up—while darker—deeper ones may encourage introspection. Our meals can also be effectively imbued with color: some hues of food will have a filling effect, while others will inspire us to move our body, which can result in losing weight.

Alongside color, you'll be able to choose different patterns, textures, fabrics and shapes that also represent the five elements. By reading this book, you will learn which ones are right for you.

Through Fashion Feng Shui® you will learn to make deliberate clothing choices that:
- flatter your appearance
- function for your lifestyle
- fulfill your essence
- fortify your intention.

Transformational Triad

The Transformational Triad illustrates the power we have to change our lives by honoring mind, body and spirit. Fashion Feng Shui® takes ancient wisdom and applies it to what is often seen as the rather mundane practice of getting dressed. In doing this, we create balance, which is essential to feel alive and well. Look at the triad again and see how each corner relates to the other. Find consistency in your mind, body and spirit, your empowered, physical and authentic self.

Throughout this book, you will be looking at how each of these affects your best clothing choices. When you marry all of them together, you can build a wardrobe that fulfils, fortifies, flatters and functions for you. One that authentically intertwines how you look with who you are, and what you want in your life.

FUNCTION - FORTIFY
INTENTION
Empowered Self
MIND

FLATTER
APPEARANCE
Physical Self
BODY

FULFILL
ESSENCE
Authentic Self
SPIRIT

What Fashion Feng Shui® Can Do for You

When the Feng Shui of your home or business is off kilter, the people who live or work there cannot flourish or make use of their full potential. Many of us face stressful situations, at home, at work or somewhere in between. These circumstances can be the result of missed opportunities, discordant relationships or stagnation. What's more, each and every aspect of an ideal life is rarely fulfilled all at once. Maybe you enjoy good health but have less money than you need: maybe your wallet is fat but you have more aches and pains than you would like. Problems can creep up on us from everywhere. Feng Shui helps clear away obstructions in daily life and, in so doing, creates a smooth path on which to walk. The list of contexts in which to apply Feng Shui cures is endless: your home and garden: an office or the entire building in which it's housed: hotels, restaurants and other commercial businesses: schools and universities: parks and public spaces: and last but not least, your own personal self. This is Fashion Feng Shui®.

Be the best you can be
You cannot control your genetics or the frame of your body. But you can control your stylistic self-expression. Becoming a more attractive man is as simple as completing a short list of action points: grooming, dressing to suit your personality, a few behavioral changes, and keeping in mind your best colors, materials, fabrics and elemental shapes and designs. Each of the elements have certain traits, which we can convert to the clothes you wear to help you radiate the energies of these elements.

Every little detail of the clothes and accessories you wear has a meaning and can make a difference in how you feel about yourself, or how others perceive you. Whether you want to up your sex appeal or recover from a business failure, start with a positive change to your appearance. Once you identify your unique qualities, you can be true to your unique self. This, in turn, lets you focus on harnessing style and cultivating self-esteem. In an increasingly competitive world, you need to be sure how to present yourself. The impression you make has a lasting effect.

FASHION FENG SHUI FOR MEN

Yin and yang

Yang colors are characterized as vibrant; yin colors are the more calming. By following the Fashion Feng Shui® incorporation of yin and yang in your dressing, you create symmetry within. When the energies of yin and yang are balanced, you feel balanced. You feel comfortable in your own skin. You feel empowered by your clothes, shoes and accessories.

When You Might Need Fashion Feng Shui®

Do you ever find yourself:
- Feeling you're somehow out of sync?
- Experiencing sudden loneliness?
- Having career problems?
- Finding it hard to interact with others?
- Having problems settling down?
- Feeling disappointed in your career results?
- Failing to keep relationships alive?
- Failing to keep relationships healthy?
- Seeking goals but unable to find one with personal resonance?
- Wanting more success?
- Wanting greater financial stability?
- Wanting to feel grounded?
- Feeling fearful of starting a relationship or a family?
- Failing to achieve what you've always wanted?
- Failing to control spending habits?
- Having problems taking action?
- Having problems following a diet?
- Seeking general quality of life but don't know where to begin?
- Wanting to experience tranquility and deeper thoughts but lack the inner peace?

These questions may be difficult to answer, but they are worth considering as you study the techniques of Fashion Feng Shui® in an effort to make life fuller, easier and more enjoyable.

Let's start by focusing on your primary essence, who you are at your very core, the inner you. Being aware of your own natural self, which is already full of energy, offers you the courage to take action. Categorizing your elemental archetype is a way to understand your authentic self. Categorizing your physiognomy is a way to see how that self shows in physical form.

The Five Elements

Let's introduce the Five Elements: Water, Wood, Fire, Earth and Metal. Each one has a direct effect on our lives. As elements, they are all different, but totally interconnected. Fashion Feng Shui® helps us see the dynamism between the elements in the world and in ourselves. Without their balancing inter-relationships, things would fall out of order in no time.

Fashion Feng Shui® personifies the elements as elemental archetypes that reflect our individual characteristics.

- The Philosopher (Water): the element of cultivating calmness
- The Pioneer (Wood): the element of feeling dynamic
- The Pleasure Seeker (Fire): the element of experiencing emotion
- The Peacemaker (Earth): the element of implementing care
- The Perfectionist (Metal): the element of creating perfection

Everyone has a mix of the elemental archetypes, and the unique combination of these energies make us the unique people we are. No person is exactly like any other. Of course, experiences shape us as well, and that all adds up to who we are today.

The following checklists will help you to clarify who you truly are when you "feel at home". None are better than others, just different. Once you've made that choice, you can then go onto customize your style so your clothes correspond to your inner feelings—the lens through which you look at the world.

If you prefer, download and print a copy of the checklists from our website: http://ffsformen.com/book-downloads

Water: The Philosopher

A man whose elemental archetype is Water loves his own environment. He may also like the wonder of the unknown. Water has no beginning and no end, filling the space it is given; similarly, this man has the ability to shape-shift, to adjust. His spirit is given to a natural flow. He is emotional and compassionate. With a rich inner world, he may be a daydreamer or someone who can build his own universe in waking life by applying what he has learned in dreams.

The Philosopher has the ability to relax others, calming them down in stressful situations. He is a natural healer. He is intelligent, with a knack for finding solutions to difficult situations. His memory never disappoints. He is a reader, a ponderer and someone who thinks before he speaks. He also likes peace and tranquility around him.

If a man lacks the Water element, he might skip over necessary deep conversations with his partner or hide his feelings. When out of balance, he may feel lost or experience insecurities. A man with a lack of Water can't support his innate self very well. Water helps to garner intellect, seek wisdom and enhance creativity. The Philosopher likes the cold weather, feeling best in the winter. He prefers evening to mornings.

Philosopher checklist

Which of the following words describe you? Check all the relevant choices and add up the total.

- ☐ Imaginative: possessing the power of imagination
- ☐ Independent: relying minimally on others for aid or support
- ☐ Introspective: being in touch with personal thoughts, feelings and expressions
- ☐ Sensitive: having greater awareness of and responsiveness to others' feelings
- ☐ Solitary: tending towards a companion-less existence
- ☐ Spiritual: taking interest in a spiritual approach towards life
- ☐ Unorthodox: not conforming to conventional behavior or rules
- ☐ Resourceful: able to find and share available resources
- ☐ Intellectual: placing a high value on intellect and knowledge, especially on an abstract level

Philosopher total: _____

Wood: The Pioneer

A man whose elemental archetype is Wood loves the outside world. He is a dynamic thinker. He likes traveling, being with others and keeping on the go. The Pioneer has a very down-to-earth demeanor. He is activity-focused, seeking to out-perform and achieve in life. He may take more risks in his working life. Others see him as very motivational, as he likes to share and encourage others. However, he is a better talker then listener.

The Pioneer is a born leader, wanting to take control and make the rules. He wants to constantly be developing himself and simply cannot sit still waiting for things to happen. An adventurist type, he likes to compete and loves challenges. On the flip-side, he can be easily bored, sometimes getting injured or struggling with his body's limitations. An antidote for this can be reading and learning, as a brain kept active can help him come to terms with any necessary slowdown or break in physical exercise.

If a man lacks the Wood element, he might be less determined in his opinions or in taking charge of situations. The Pioneer needs space in his home to relax and to wind down. His favorite season is spring for all its new life and the sprouting of nature. He prefers getting up early to staying up late.

Pioneer checklist

Which of the following words describe you? Check all the relevant choices and add up the total.

- ☐ Dynamic: being highly flexible in your thoughts and actions
- ☐ Trustworthy: easily being trusted with huge responsibilities
- ☐ Ambitious: desiring and usually achieving success or power
- ☐ Assertive: being confident and direct in claiming your rights or forwarding your views
- ☐ Direct: thinking and acting in a straightforward, frank
- ☐ Youthful: having the appearance of freshness and vigor
- ☐ Growth promoting: embracing the process of growing into your life
- ☐ Evolving: increasing success in your private and professional life gradually but steadily
- ☐ Health-conscious: keeping conscious of your fitness and overall physical health

Pioneer total: _____

Fire: The Pleasure Seeker

A man whose elemental archetype is Fire embodies the peaks and joys in his own life. People love to have this charismatic type around. He draws others in like nobody else can. What can be so appealing about him is his artistic, passionate side. Plus, he is very self-confidant, a naturally proud soul who is pleased with his own successes. His outlook is positive and warm. He is courteous, expressive, good at complimenting others in his speech, maybe a little flirtatious.

The Pleasure Seeker wants to have fun in life with his partner, his friends and family. He will always see opportunities to arrange outings, dinners and parties: his invitations simply cannot be refused. The Pleasure Seeker welcomes expressions of gratitude from his loved ones. He can change his emotions rapidly in certain situations, but he will always be energetic and kind to others. The Pleasure Seeker is not very good on his own and can become easily lonely. Once out of balance, he can become a bit impulsive and act without thinking a situation through.

When a man lacks Fire, he is less able to convey his true passions or easily manifest gentle or spontaneous reactions. Communicating through his heart or sending messages of kindness to loved ones is not as easy as he would like it to be—it just doesn't come out of him naturally. Fire will help to open up his heart. If a man lacks the Fire element he is likely struggling to experience fun. He is often too serious, and can be living an exceedingly worried life. He may be prone to have little confidence and can be agitated when his life becomes less happy. A Pleasure Seeker feels at his best at midday and prefers summer to all the other seasons.

Pleasure Seeker checklist

Which of the following words describe you? Check all the relevant choices and add up the total.

- ☐ Fascinating: attracting others
- ☐ Affectionate: being able to show affection easily
- ☐ Understanding: having good knowledge of a particular skill or how to handle particular issues
- ☐ Enthusiastic: possessing an eagerness that impassions you as a listener and a doer
- ☐ Entertaining: exercising hospitality and providing generously for guests
- ☐ Fun-loving: enjoying life to the fullest and with great pleasure
- ☐ Impulsive: acting in the moment
- ☐ Mischievous: loving to play—and to play innocent
- ☐ Passionate: having and expressing strong feelings in an intense manner

Pleasure Seeker total: _____

Earth: The Peacemaker

A man whose elemental archetype is Earth embodies stability. With a down to earth attitude, he cares a lot for his family and puts the well-being of others before himself. This element is between seasons. The Peacemaker is very connected to his relatives, his co-workers, his roots and tradition. He loves his home—it is his castle. He is also a very good administrator, and performs well in office jobs. He prefers to keep to himself, holding onto his thoughts and beliefs.

The Peacemaker actively cares for others. He is very generous with his time and money, looking out for others, nurturing, cooking and feeding them, sometimes even spoiling them. Others can trust the Peacemaker in his actions: he will not fail or abandon anybody. If he is your buddy, trust that he will stay a loyal friend for life.

One thing that may be difficult to live with, if the Peacemaker is a colleague or a partner, is his stubbornness. The Peacemaker represents himself through reliable and trustworthy actions. Loosening up can only happen by adding Fire elemental colors and styles to his attire. This is the cure to resolving excessive firmness, as the Fire element melts this down a bit and makes a person more flexible. If a man lacks the Earth element, he has tendencies to be more selfish and possessive. He may not to listen to others' opinions and be very self-willed. He likes his afternoons and loves the late summer.

Peacemaker checklist

Which of the following words describe you? Check all the relevant choices and add up the total.

- ☐ Selfless: putting concerns of others above your own interests
- ☐ Reliable: being someone others can depend on consistently
- ☐ Caring: someone who puts others before him or herself
- ☐ Committed: tending to take charge and deliver results in a practical manner
- ☐ Compliant: surrendering readily to others in a considerate way
- ☐ Diplomatic: dealing tactfully with sensitive matters or people
- ☐ Grounded: being well-rooted and down-to-earth
- ☐ Health-focused: being involved with all aspects of personal health
- ☐ Responsible: possessing great dependability as someone who can take control

Peacemaker total: _____

Metal: The Perfectionist

A man whose elemental archetype is Metal man can be trusted with numbers and computation. This well-mannered, impeccably put-together type has an air of sophistication about him. He is a good organizer and craves structure. The Perfectionist loves tastefulness in interior design, eating out, art, music and clothing, preferring quality over quantity. He has high expectations of his earning power and always wants to achieve the ultimate in whatever he is capable of. The Perfectionist has great leadership qualities and believes "the devil is in the details."

Because of his own disciplined determination, he cannot understand colleagues, partners or friends who prefer more frivolity or tranquility in their lives. He requires order in his life. If he cannot achieve it, chaos is sure to be lurking around the corner. Similarly, when he feels under the weather, he may perceive his life as being in shambles. At times like this, he may be unable to cope and need help. Others need to step in and lend a hand, whatever the nature of the perceived crisis.

FASHION FENG SHUI FOR MEN

Perfectionist checklist

Which of the following words describe you? Check all the relevant choices and add up the total.

- ☐ Analytical: gathering all the facts before taking action
- ☐ Accurate: advocating the correct, precise handling of private and professional matters
- ☐ Cultivated: valuing culture
- ☐ Distinctive: having a unique quality in your style and appearance
- ☐ Elegant: being graceful and stylish in appearance or manner
- ☐ Meticulous: showing extreme care for details, notably through a manicured appearance
- ☐ Refined: paying attention to details
- ☐ Organized: arranging your life very methodically
- ☐ Reserved: being formal or self-restrained in manner or how you relate to others

Perfectionist total: _____

Identify Your Essence

So, you now have an overview of the different elemental archetypes and their personal traits. Let's explore a little further.

The Five Element Personality Test gives you a practical tool for getting in touch with your genuine self, which, in turn, lets you create a genuine expression of yourself. The test offers insight into your strengths and weaknesses and, in so doing, reflects how you currently present your inner self to the outer world. Its aim is to help you understand more about your primary essence. Your essence is your archetypal elemental design—it's what you are made of and what you are all about. Essence is the very center of your energy, your drive, your preferences, your inner self. Understanding which archetype you are helps you to grasp the flow of life.

To find out what your essence is in Fashion Feng Shui® terms, you can identify personally relevant points on our essence checklist. Once you identify these points, tally up how many are present and, from there, determine how much of one archetypes or another is represented in your essence.

The Five Element Personality Test
Check as many of the items from each of the five elements that describe you. The element with the most checks is your primary essence, while the one with the second most is your influencing essence. This is an excellent start, but keep in mind that a more in-depth analysis always deepens your knowledge and ensures better results.

FASHION FENG SHUI FOR MEN

If you prefer, download and print a copy of this test from our website: http://ffsformen.com/book-downloads

Water: The Philosopher

Which of these words and phrases speak to you?
- ☐ Forgets everything around himself.
- ☐ Is a deep thinker with creative abilities.
- ☐ Considered.
- ☐ Thoughtful.
- ☐ Observant.
- ☐ Wise.
- ☐ Forgiving.
- ☐ Patient.
- ☐ Serious intellectual.
- ☐ Reflective.
- ☐ Truthful.
- ☐ Persevering.
- ☐ Isolated.
- ☐ Discreet.
- ☐ Peaceful.
- ☐ Philosophical.
- ☐ Stubborn.
- ☐ Solitary.

Which of the following sentences could you hear yourself saying?
- ☐ I like speaking freely and deep from within.
- ☐ I like to be calm and love winters.
- ☐ I like being with my own thoughts and don't mind tranquility.

The Philosopher total: _____

Wood: The Pioneer

Which of these words and phrases speak to you?
- ☐ Working mode, always growing.
- ☐ Physically active.
- ☐ A born entrepreneur.
- ☐ Driven.
- ☐ Focused.
- ☐ Active.
- ☐ Realistic.
- ☐ Fast.
- ☐ Argumentative.
- ☐ Impatient.
- ☐ Competitive.
- ☐ Direct.
- ☐ Tough.
- ☐ Resolute.
- ☐ Pushy.
- ☐ Bold.
- ☐ Assured.
- ☐ Self-important.
- ☐ Dynamic.
- ☐ Energetic.
- ☐ Forward-thinking.

Which of the following sentences could you hear yourself saying?
- ☐ I like to initiate changes in my life.
- ☐ I like action-oriented progress.
- ☐ I like to reach goals in my life.

The Pioneer total: _____

FASHION FENG SHUI FOR MEN

Fire: The Pleasure Seeker

Which of these words and phrases speak to you?
- ☐ Radiates charisma.
- ☐ Loves partying.
- ☐ Caresses those around him.
- ☐ Easily fosters friendships.
- ☐ Spontaneous.
- ☐ Passionate.
- ☐ Easily distracted.
- ☐ Optimistic.
- ☐ Flexible.
- ☐ Flirtatious.
- ☐ Charming.
- ☐ Witty.
- ☐ Commutative.
- ☐ Enthusiastic.
- ☐ Adaptable.
- ☐ Natural.
- ☐ Magnetic.
- ☐ Unpredictable.
- ☐ Lively.
- ☐ Changeable.
- ☐ Expressive.
- ☐ Mischievous.
- ☐ Talkative.

Which of the following sentences could you hear yourself saying?
- ☐ I am intensely engaged and passionate-minded.
- ☐ I live to the fullest and laugh a lot.
- ☐ I easily get noticed and love it.

The Pleasure Seeker total: _____

Earth: The Peacemaker

Which of these words and phrases speak to you?
- ☐ Keeps caring for others.
- ☐ Makes friends for life.
- ☐ Has a knack for keeping the peace.
- ☐ Nurturing.
- ☐ Down-to-earth.
- ☐ Comforting.
- ☐ Involved.
- ☐ Corporate.
- ☐ Considerate.
- ☐ Hesitant.
- ☐ Guarded.
- ☐ Consistent.
- ☐ Concerned.
- ☐ Cautious.
- ☐ Devoted.
- ☐ Committed.
- ☐ Steady.
- ☐ Unhurried.
- ☐ Even-tempered.
- ☐ Comfortable.
- ☐ Reliable.
- ☐ Useful.

Which of the following sentences could you hear yourself saying?
- ☐ I like being grounded in who I am.
- ☐ I like taking care of others and attending to them.
- ☐ I like a down-to-earth approach in life.

The Peacemaker total: _____

FASHION FENG SHUI FOR MEN

Metal: The Perfectionist

Which of these words and phrases speak to you?
- ☐ Strives for perfectionism.
- ☐ Is refined and elegant.
- ☐ Has expensive taste.
- ☐ Orderly.
- ☐ Meticulous.
- ☐ Precise.
- ☐ Uncluttered.
- ☐ Well-dressed.
- ☐ Idealistic.
- ☐ Discreet.
- ☐ Refined.
- ☐ Tidy.
- ☐ Analytical.
- ☐ Aloof.
- ☐ Organized.
- ☐ Systematic.
- ☐ Distant.
- ☐ Formal.
- ☐ Logical.
- ☐ Well-groomed.
- ☐ Elegant.
- ☐ Well-mannered.

Which of the following sentences could you hear yourself saying?
- ☐ I demand precision of others and myself.
- ☐ I like quality and structure in my life.
- ☐ I like the finer things in life.

The Perfectionist total: _____

Your Authentic Self

Having explored the elemental archetypes, you have made a concrete start in the search for your authentic self. By reflecting on yourself, digging a little deeper than you normally would, you can get in touch with your essence. With the help of Fashion Feng Shui®, you can better understand the whole you, someone closer to who you were as a little boy. Looking back, you may realize how many habits, self-made or borrowed, may have picked up at a young age and continue to practice to this day. Some adults are fortunate in that they do not mimic others too much—copying too many behaviors doesn't permit authenticity to shine through. But even for those of us who have, Fashion Feng Shui® provides a concrete framework to help us get in touch with our own identity and stay close to it.

For instance, if you are more of a Philosopher and one or both parents are Pioneers, you may have struggled with their action-oriented mind-set, always pushing you towards one of their own goals. All you may have wanted was to stay relaxed, perhaps reading, listen to music or writing a poem. Your parents may not have understood you and your needs, wondering what would become of you. The reverse could be true: maybe your parents were very laid-back, pondering types, while you sought to stay active from morning till night.

Consider another example: maybe your parents have/had a lot of the Perfectionist in them and therefore wanted your life to be totally regimented and controlled. If you are a Philosopher, you may never have really understood their structure-focused methods, and just gone along without protest. However, without realizing it, they brought balance in you, helping organize your daily life and learning to cope with routines.

Physical Appearance

Your soul speaks from and through your body. Your physiognomy, inherent coloring and body shape are included in the appearance section of the Transformational Triad. Dressing your physical appearance flatters the external part of you.

Complete the physiognomy and body shape checklists below to evaluate your appearance. If you prefer, download and print a copy of the checklists from our website: http://ffsformen.com/book-downloads

Water physiognomy and body shape checklist
Which of the following physical traits apply to you? Check all the relevant choices and add up the total:
- ☐ Overall deep coloring: dark hair, medium to dark skin tone, dark blue or brown eyes.
- ☐ High forehead: a naturally high hairline.
- ☐ Eye circles: dark circles under eyes.
- ☐ Protruding chin: a chin that sticks out.
- ☐ Large boned frame: large body frame is a skeletal structure that is bigger—wider—or denser than average.
- ☐ Asymmetric frame: upper half of body is smaller than lower half.
- ☐ Drawling speech: a slow manner of speaking.
- ☐ Choppy speech: using a lot of "um"s and "uh"s while speaking.
- ☐ Relaxed gait: walking at a slow, leisurely pace.

The Philosopher total: _____

FASHION FENG SHUI FOR MEN

Wood physiognomy and body shape checklist
Which of the following physical traits apply to you? Check all the relevant choices and add up the total:
- ☐ Strong brow line: prominently shaped eyebrows.
- ☐ Prominent jawline: a strong jaw.
- ☐ Long limbs: arms and legs that are too long for most jackets and trousers.
- ☐ Athletic frame: a very fit, toned body.
- ☐ Columnar frame: a rectangular-shaped body.
- ☐ Powerful voice: speech that uses high volume and intensity.
- ☐ Direct speech: speaking in a straightforward manner.
- ☐ Determined gait: walking at a fast pace

The Pioneer total: _____

Fire physiognomy and body shape checklist
Which of the following physical traits apply to you? Check all the relevant choices and add up the total:
- ☐ Pinkish colored skin: delicate skin type.
- ☐ Sparkling eyes: eyes show the emotions from inside.
- ☐ Specific facial features: like a tip-tilted nose.
- ☐ Clear smile: laughing, showing of dimples.
- ☐ Curly hair: hair is unruly and wild.
- ☐ Inverted triangle body shape: wider shoulders and narrow hips and thighs.
- ☐ Active voice: very lively and passionate.
- ☐ Animated speech: full of life and energy.
- ☐ Spring in the step: walks with little jumps in between.

The Pleasure Seeker total: _____

Earth physiognomy and body shape checklist

Which of the following physical traits apply to you? Check all the relevant choices and add up the total:

- ☐ Full lips: upper and lower lips are full.
- ☐ Round cheeks: full cheeks.
- ☐ Solid upper arms: firm upper arms.
- ☐ Firm body shape: a robust appearance.
- ☐ Sturdy construction: your body frame is large or extra large.
- ☐ Square characteristics: a square-shaped chin, for instance.
- ☐ Deliberate speech: carefully weighed and considered words.
- ☐ Melodic voice: speech that is harmonious sounding.
- ☐ Relaxed gait: walking slowly

The Peacemaker total: _____

Metal physiognomy and body shape checklist

Which of the following physical traits apply to you? Check all the relevant choices and add up the total:

- ☐ Pale coloring: if your complexion is light overall.
- ☐ Curved nose: if a bend or bump is present in the profile of your nose bridge.
- ☐ High cheekbones: high cheekbones are closer to the eyes than low cheekbones.
- ☐ Delicate features: an overall slim, fine-boned frame.
- ☐ Small build: not too tall.
- ☐ Melancholic voice: a pensive way of speaking.
- ☐ Cultivated speech: a refined way of talking.
- ☐ Upright gait: walking with head held straight forward.

The Perfectionist total: _____

Essential Dressing

To feel confident in and about yourself, give all the advised clothes—their different colors, materials, fabrics, elemental shapes and designs—a try. These selections are meant to provide you with renewed energy to focus on present and future challenges. From personal life events to corporate functions, you deserve to appear, feel and be self-assured.

Note that you may experience a situation in which you had planned everything down to the last detail, but still felt you lacked the right look. Fashion Feng Shui® would respond to this by observing that your style did not correspond to your essence. Often a mismatch like this is the only reason to make you feel uneasy. Dressing according to your essence is the key to your authentic ability. It also profoundly affects how others relate to and treat you.

Choose from the selections below, firstly for your essence. Adjust accordingly for your appearance if required.

How to dress The Philosopher

Expression:	unique.
Colors:	bordeaux, black, dark-blue, ultramarine, dark green.
Patterns:	abstract, psychedelic, paisley.
Styles:	avant-garde, fluid, creative.
Fabrics:	rayon, jersey, wool-blend.
Signature piece:	wide-legged trousers and a loose-fitting jacket in dark blue, green or black, finished off with an avant-garde-style shirt and chunky black Ankle-high boots.

FASHION FENG SHUI FOR MEN

How to dress The Pioneer

Expression:	sporty, casual.
Colors:	all greens and blues, ranging from jade to aqua.
Patterns:	stripes, solids, botanicals.
Styles:	refreshing yet natural.
Fabrics:	linen, pure cotton, denim, jersey.
Signature piece:	a linen jacket with a cotton striped shirt or T-shirt and a pair of chinos or jeans.

How to dress The Pleasure Seeker

Expression:	extravagant, flashy.
Colors:	red, light-bordeaux, yellow, bright-orange, purple.
Patterns:	pointed collars in shirts or jackets, diamond shape.
Styles:	very colorful, embellished.
Fabrics:	leather, satin, wool.
Signature piece:	leather jacket, satin shirt, diamond shaped patterned sweater, a colorful pair of pants or trousers.

How to dress The Peacemaker

Expression:	traditional.
Colors:	khaki, burnt-orange, orange-red, sand, brown.
Patterns:	tartans, checks.
Styles:	timeless, casual-suiting.
Fabrics:	tweed, nubuck, natural materials, textured.
Signature piece:	a classic suit in nubuck fabric with a check-patterned shirt, accompanied by classic dark brown suede Oxford shoes.

How to dress The Perfectionist

Expression:	luxurious, sophisticated.
Colors:	monochromatic schemes, pastels, white, metallics.
Patterns:	polka dots on accessories such as ties and socks, solids.
Styles:	precise, detailed, structured.
Fabrics:	cashmere and other specialty wools, often expensive.
Signature piece:	A classy three-piece designer woolen suit with a cotton dress shirt in a coordinated color, bow tie or tie with a polka-dot pattern, elegant socks in a coordinated hue and a pair of Chelsea boots.

Case Studies

The following section provides profiles and case studies of different men. Each is categorized according to his elemental archetype—that is, which of Feng Shui's five elements is most present in his essence. As you read through them, identify which element or elements most resonate with you.

Some of these situations may be familiar to you: others may feel a world away from your reality. Regardless, the hope is that you can learn from the guidance given in these hypothetical scenarios and apply it to your own life.

Charles
Age 48, divorced with no children. Director of a small successful firm, has proven to be a reasonable leader, though has issues with a few members of his staff.

Presentation
Overall good looks, fair complexion, but appears a bit tired and in need of refreshing. He shows no sign of the confident businessman he is.

Observation
An elegant, cultured man who enjoys the latest gadgets and the finer things in life, Charles clearly has a lot of Metal. However, his daily dressing does not reflect this. Nor does it show how much he values perfection.

Feedback
The first step is to declutter his wardrobe, including all accessories, such as shoes, attaché cases and other leather accessories.

After searching for his elemental archetype, which is mostly The Perfectionist (metal), we find that chaos has filled Charles's life. He is under various pressures. He lacks incentives to be more proactive and to reflect on his decisions. He needs to build in more balance into his life's daily routine.

Advice
Working with Charles through the Fashion Feng Shui® process we see that his authentic identity is the successful, impeccably put-together businessman. We also recognize a dire need to restructure his life. His wardrobe needs an audit. We sort through all his clothes and accessories, showing him how to combine what remains and what to look for when replacing items cast aside. We draw up a wardrobe planner showing him the latest trends in fashion, where to get them and how to make a statement with them. Since his best time is evening, we advise him to set aside time then to reflect on his day's progress and make his resolutions. We point out that autumn is his best season to launch a new project. We also advise him to recognize his Perfectionist traits in his dealings with others. His Perfectionist thinking leads to struggles with some employees whose characters are opposite to his own. Realizing his own ways can help him empathize with others and therefore create a better work environment with these employees.

Progress
Charles becomes more committed to following our wardrobe plan. He proves he can build up a workable wardrobe, with space for replacements. He meets his goals more easily. His employees see him as the leader, aware of his aims for perfection. His relationships improved and he feels like he has a new lease on life.

John
Age 34, single. Tour guide and world traveler.

Presentation
John lives in the present, but has lost his spirit. With unmissable red hair, he was once the center of attention. His life was so full of exciting adventures and fun that he didn't have a chance to finish schooling, though he wanted to. Today he is a stressed-out comfort eater, and his body shows it. He needs to focus on letting go of his excess weight and, in so doing, find more fulfillment and stability.

Observation
Working with John, we learn his elemental archetype is a mixture of The Pleasure Seeker (Fire) and The Pioneer (Wood), with The Peacemaker (Earth) as his influencing essence. His personality is vibrant, but he needs to discover what fulfills him. Although work keeps him going, his passion seems to lie elsewhere. We challenge him to find his true passion and to make a living that way.

Feedback
John is a people person, but he needs to put himself first so he can find satisfaction in life. A mindful approach to his daily routine is a solution. A better diet would be a major first step. He also needs more rest: fatigue bothers him, blocking all potential for pleasure and contentment. His innate Fire energy must be welcomed to come to the surface, allowing him to feel reborn and exhilarated.

Advice
We advise John to un-clutter his whole house, paying special attention to his wardrobe. Over the years, in an effort to hold onto his past, he has accumulated too much. A streamlined wardrobe highlights items that need repairing. We sort through the worn-out pieces. We go shopping with him to point out elements of fun that can be used to generate more love and life around him. Incorporating trends into his new clothes and accessories keeps his wardrobe up to date. We produce a style schematic that he can study and apply to get out of the stalemate.

FASHION FENG SHUI FOR MEN

Advocating he get back in touch with his motivated self, we show him a few classic, sporty pieces that can infuse action-oriented energy into his outfits. We discuss weight loss and consequently promote active wear, which should help him feel more athletically inclined. We introduce aqua blue and green, Wood hues that can foster a more energetic lifestyle. Considering his current job does not fulfill him, we suggest he use his experience to give public talks about the many countries he has journeyed to as a tour guide. Because Earth represents equanimity, we recommend he wear some earth tones, supporting his intentions to create a more stable life. We point out, too, how adding some of The Perfectionist into his daily attire can attract business opportunities.

Progress

John's life undergoes enormous changes. Contentment enters into his whole existence. The de-cluttering creates more freedom and opportunities in his life, allowing him to acknowledge his weight problem. He starts living a healthier life, and the results become ready visible. People started noticing him again.

Leonard
Age 39, single. Works in politics.

Presentation
Behind a pale complexion that contrasts with dark eyes and hair, Leonard carries a lot of stress. He worries about his past failed relationships. He sleeps very little. He is slightly overweight and has tried unsuccessfully to exercise on weekends. He doesn't manage to find time to party either, which is something he used to love. He has a busy job and would like to find a way to infuse creativity in his profession, but he doesn't dare explore those possibilities—financial commitments for maintaining his house are too pressing.

Observation
We first meet Leonard online. Via video chat, we see a tired-looking, disillusioned man who is nevertheless very sweet and gentle in his demeanor. Straight away, we recognize his elemental archetype of The Philosopher (Water), observing how right he is to wish for more creativity in his life. We answer his various questions, schedule a day to work in person with him, and give him an assignment. Using words and images cut out from magazines, he must create one collage that reflects how he presently sees himself. A second collage is to depict his intentions, showing where he wants to be in the next five years.

Feedback
It is clear that Leonard's creative mind needs some waking-up so he can discover his true essence. Water energy makes for creative, sensible and reflective people. This emotional type of man values social contact and attracts others to him.

Advice
The results make it clear that Leonard wants to become active again, and he wants to be noticed and loved along the way. That means he needs more of The Pleasure Seeker (Fire) and The Pioneer (Wood) in his clothing, which we show him how to incorporate through a style portfolio. The way he completes his assignment amazes us. His first

FASHION FENG SHUI FOR MEN

collage shows a sad, lonely man in the middle of a crowd. The second collage is full of colors and interesting, fun-loving places, which so much suit his intention of becoming more vibrant and loving to others. How creative he is with the boards reveals an artist hiding within. We recommend his creativity be explored outside work and advise him to look for a course or some structured way to discover which sort of creative path he should pursue.

Progress

By our second meeting, also online, Leonard is enrolled in an art course. There are new developments in his career, which appear after he contacts his party leaders to discuss how he wants to grow in his role. Other opportunities to work in education are offered to him, and he decides to accept the new challenge. It will intensify his deep wish to implement creativity in his work. We hope that his new challenge in education will offer him the fulfillment he has always desired.

Frederick
Age 54, divorced with three adult children. Business owner.

Presentation
A sturdy man with brown hair and a medium-toned complexion, his appearance gives an impression of The Peacemaker (Earth) and a little of The Philosopher (Water). His daily routine sounds very much one The Perfectionist would love. Frederick owns and runs four different businesses, all of which he handles very seriously. He is always working: his barely existent private life is postponed to the final hours of the night. His youth was characterized by a lot of moving around. Having divorced parents and lacking domestic consistency, he was mostly raised by Grandma.

Observation
Frederick desperately needs to feel grounded again. He is wondering if he should maybe let go of some of his business and has his children take over. He needs to start trusting his own gut feeling again and reflect on life a bit more. Finding his inner soul may prove difficult. For years, he was entirely dedicated to work, overlooking the value of bonding with his children. In fact, he was not part of their lives for many years. They loved him for the hard-working father he was and how he took care of them all financially. However, he had no idea what kept them going strong or happy.

Feedback
If Frederick could turn his life around by implementing the traits of his core essence, The Philosopher, specifically listening to his gut feelings, he would achieve more calmness and well-being.

Advice
We identify The Philosopher as his elemental archetype. It shocks him that his way of life, which is highly organized and planned, totally contradicts his inner self. We sketch out a roadmap to a new lifestyle, which includes yoga classes, library visits and culture-rich holidays. His wardrobe is in need of total transformation. We find useful items to

include in his style schematic. By no means can he suddenly drop the reins of his businesses, for this would surely affect his health. Yet, we advise him to gradually pass leadership on to two of his children who are interested and already involved in the business.

Progress

Contacting Frederick again after a couple weeks, we meet a different man. The deep thinker surfaced. He had gradually introduced all our advice into his life, although it was not easy. But the biggest surprise of all is that his ex-wife and all his children are now working in his businesses. This helps him grow into his own, while also letting go of some of his work stress. That, in turn, rekindles a romance with his ex-wife. She loves his free spirit, now surfacing but, for various reasons, hidden all his life.

Brian
Age 62, widower. Early retiree.

Presentation
Brian is a former hippie, unhappily living on his own ever since his wife died. His only child is married, with a family of his own. Slim-built, he has fair hair, a large unkempt mustache and a generally scruffy appearance. He loves classic films and embraces their cultural ethos. He rides everywhere on his old Harley-Davidson. He is most concerned about love for his fellow man and taking care of the planet. A fast lifestyle is strange to him, and he would feel most comfortable a society of non-materialism.

Observation
We first meet Brian online. He says straight away that he heard of Fashion Feng Shui® from a friend and that it had opened up all sorts of opportunities for him. He asks what he himself could get out of it. A lot, if that's what he needs, is the reply. His laughing and joking reflect his jovial spirit. He does not aspire to sophistication, but is seeking a bit of elevation in how he lives.

Advice
Brian is a happy soul—from the outside. Inside, he feels lonely and unaccepted. Over time, his own hippie allure has come to fade. It is time for some structure and a clean, fresh look. It is clear that The Pleasure Seeker is Brian's main essence. We explain to him how the elements link us to the world. Brian, a free spirit, has an innate connection to nature, and there is no way he should compromise that. What we want for him is to see his shortcomings in how he tends to both his surroundings and his own appearance. We create a balanced style portfolio for him so transforming his appearance won't feel like such a challenge. We also encourage him to spruce up his house.

Progress
By the time he has digested the initial Fashion Feng Shui® information, he should be ready for the next step. His predominantly scruffy

FASHION FENG SHUI FOR MEN

appearance could do with some help. It would make him feel more tranquil and grounded. We start a plan for his grooming and make an appointment to sort out his wardrobe and go shopping with him. Once we take steps to improve his grooming and wardrobe, he starts getting more respect from others right away.

Jonathan
Age 40, lives with his girlfriend. Associate corporate banker with potential career growth.

Presentation
Jonathan is a go-getter with a reasonable approach to dressing for work. Outside the bank, however, it is a different story. He loves to watch team sports with his old university friends and meet up at a favorite bar with them. It appears as though he does not want to grow up.

Observation
Because of his busy schedule, we start our consultation online and ask him to send us some pictures. He definitely dresses like a banker, but not very spectacularly. On his days off, he is the complete opposite. He does not care one bit how he looks, and actually seems to be reverting to the rebellious student he once was. There is nothing intrinsically wrong with that, as many men don't want to mature until they're in their forties. But in seeking our advice, Jonathan was clearly seeking change.

Feedback
Before his consultation, we send him the pre-consultation questionnaire and arrange a video chat to learn more about his personality and his intentions. Gradually, it becomes apparent that he simply does not know how to find time for everything: working life, romantic relationship, friends. He wants it all. We decide to focus first on his style at work and then turn to his wardrobe overall.

Advice
At work, Jonathan assumes the role of The Perfectionist. He is comfortable with strategic planning and maintaining formal relationships with clients, but his work suits do not reflect these traits. Suits can differ in texture, design or fit, and all aspects of the right suit for your essential design are important for the best results. A rational thinker, Jonathan can report on his own personality by answering our questions. We ask him for his budget for buying new clothes and accessories to form a

plan for preparing a shopping trip with him. We then plan a visit for him to a tailoring shop to have two high-quality suits made.

We discover that in his private life, chaos is rampant. Jonathan struggles to find structure, seeking to be more proactive and to grow out of the weekend university rebel. We find that introducing Wood energy (The Pioneer) can help him in this regard. We therefore create two separate style schematics, one for professional life and one for private. We encourage him to impress his girlfriend and his friends with a totally different approach to dressing. Before long, he visits a tailor in his hometown. With the guidance of his style schematic, he is able to invest in clothes that help him get where he wants to be.

Progress
Jonathan does not speak about his girlfriend until we communicate with him online a few weeks later. In fact, it is the first topic he brings up. He says that she had started to admire his new ways and wants to be together more often. He also gets positive feedback at work. We never advise Jonathan to adjust his behavior, but he does in fact modify his lifestyle without compromising the laughter and fun he shares with his mates.

Mike
43, divorced with no kids. Accountant for a large firm.

Presentation
Mike divorced his wife after coming to terms with being gay. Working for years as an accountant for a large firm, he has made numbers his life, and his knack for them comes in handy when he gambles on Saturdays. He had a good upbringing, and still shares a meal at his parents' house every Sunday. His elemental essence is The Pioneer (Wood) and his influencing essence is The Peacemaker (Earth). In the unkempt, faded clothes he wears, he looks about ten years older than he actually is.

Observation
Mike appears tidy but old-fashioned. He comes across as dry, if not rather lifeless. Since coming out, he has not managed to find his place in society or to find ways to socialize more. But he is unable to find the time and the place to make that happen because of the rigid demands of his profession. He is very dependable and action-oriented, as well as good at supervising and observing. But it seems he needs to enjoy his professional life as much as his private, both sorely lacking vibrancy.

Feedback
Working with Mike is easy. Cooking emerges as a latent hobby, though he has no incentive to indulge it. He is totally engulfed by his work and how others judge him. His life needs to be imbued once again with space and freedom of movement. Elemental shapes and designs that incorporate The Pleasure Seeker (Fire) as well as The Perfectionist (Metal) would be of help.

Advice
With our guidance, Mike identifies his intentions. They are not natural for him to discover: he had to hide his true feelings for years. This has caused him to become a loner, a sort of outcast people are not inclined to get acquainted with. No wonder he does not sparkle. That begins to change, however, when he learns about The Pleasure Seeker (Fire).

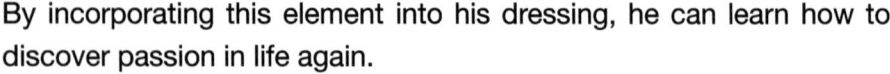
FASHION FENG SHUI FOR MEN

By incorporating this element into his dressing, he can learn how to discover passion in life again.

Progress

We eventually hear how Mike begins inviting his parents to his house on Sundays and relishes cooking for them. He seems so much more alive, and he isn't going to stop here. He is now ready to show his true self to the world, and does not seem to be at all afraid of it.

Transform Yourself through Fashion Feng Shui®

Now that you've made it to here, you may realize how this innovative person-focused style system could be of great benefit for you. It doesn't matter whether you are in the beginning of your career, searching for a partner, or finding answers to why you don't always feel right when it matters most. You want to show the world outside who you really are, and our innovative person-focused style system can help you feel balanced from within. While our essence is not prone to change, our intentions can change over time. What we wear and how we wear it can catalyze those changes.

Essential energy is the energetic lens through which you see the world. It shapes the relationship between your center and your natural emotional self. Your behavior is part of your unique essence, which is truly only yours. Essential energy is unconsciously expressed. Intentional energy, however, is consciously expressed. It is the energy attached to what you want to possess, including the goals you envision reaching. Different colors, materials, fabrics and elemental shapes and designs can be effectively applied to enhance your life. Wardrobe management and stylization play a dynamic role in your personal development. You can dress in ways that are conductive to concrete success.

Implementing the five elements

Introducing each element into your life can have different results. We often need different energies during the course of our lives, and Fashion Feng Shui® can help us to implement these energies when they're needed. Look at what each element represents, and you'll know in which part of your life you'll need that energy. Which of the element archetypes could be of good use to you right now?

- **The Philosopher** can help you tap into creativity.
- **The Pioneer** can help you reinvent yourself.
- **The Pleasure Seeker** can help you become animated and fun-loving.

- **The Peacemaker** can help you become more grounded and practical.
- **The Perfectionist** can help you get organized and attract prosperity.

Color

Fashion Feng Shui® helps you discover the colors that will work most effectively to enhance your mood and awaken your passion. Wear the brighter colors of Fire and you communicate a stronger message. Wear the warmer colors of Earth or Wood and you feel warmer. Wear the pastel shades of Metal and you convey more elegance. Wear the darker hues of Water and create calmness.

Color is also the first thing you notice when you look at another person. Not only is it important because of its effect on facial complexion, but also for its ability to create optical illusions. Your Fashion Feng Shui® consultation will help you choose colors that highlight your assets and subdue your less favorable features. Are your shoulders narrower than you would like? Do you wish your legs were longer? Do you find yourself too tall? Tricks with color can address these concerns.

WATER

WOOD

FIRE

EARTH

METAL

Detailing

Fashion Feng Shui® consultations reveal exactly which pieces in a wardrobe help express your innate self. The process is not oppressive or tedious. It helps you pay attention to detail in your attire, something that many people—often men-have let fall by the wayside in recent decades. This helps you enter into the world with a much better self-understanding and self-image. In turn, you cultivate more self-respect. You find yourself more confident to stand up to everyday life's challenges. Silhouettes that flatter your natural body frame will enhance your overall look. Fashion Feng Shui® advises which lines, cuts and shapes best suit you and which are best to avoid.

Stylish living means something different to each of us. Regardless of your personal elemental archetype, it is important to choose appropriate clothes and to make sure they fit properly. But having the right wardrobe is not just about fashion. It is also about knowing how to dress your inner self.

Positive feedback

How you wear your clothes is a major way to create a good first impression. It has a direct, immediate effect on what others think of you. It is true that the better you are dressed, the more respect and positivity you will find come your way. That said, just because you work in an environment where the dress code is conservative, you don't need to conform mindlessly to the point of boredom. Fashion Feng Shui® encourages you to let your own unique personality radiate. Dare to stand out, even in business attire. Live by your style schematic and success will follow.

Grooming

Men often have a morning personal care regime, but it frequently ends before noon. Fashion Feng Shui® promotes good hygiene and self-care throughout the day. Moisturizing your face and using sunscreen make a huge difference in keeping you younger-looking. Have a toothbrush and a nice scent on hand, especially for use after lunch. Polish your shoes regularly. Crisp shirts and clean socks are musts. Visit a barber or hairdresser every four weeks for maintenance. Get a professional facial once in a while. Good grooming speaks for itself—not just because of its effects on your skin, hair and attire, but also because of the glow of the successes it brings you.

Your wardrobe

The contents of your closet are often a mix of attire for various seasons, and that can present a challenge in the early morning if you're rushing to get to work. In the Northern Hemisphere, set aside time in early October to remove the summer items from your wardrobe, store them elsewhere and replace them with winter items. Do the reverse process in early April. This twice-yearly ritual will keep your wardrobe season-appropriate. If you use it as an opportunity to discard pieces that have stopped reflecting your elemental energy, you'll also find space to fit in new clothing and accessories that express your inner truth.

Dress Your Intention

To fulfill your dreams, harmonize from within. While still honoring your essence and appearance, you can pull in aspects of another archetype based on your intention. Ask yourself: which of the elemental archetypes can help me reach—and, if necessary, re-orientate—my goals?

If your goal is **to be more intense**, wear more Water clothing details. In Water: we wear styles that allow the expression of our individualism.

If your goal is **to act or do more**, add Wood clothing details. In Wood: we wear styles that allow us to act freely.

If your goal is **to have more fun**, wear more Fire clothing details. In Fire: we wear styles that draw attention and attraction to ourselves.

If your goal is **to belong more**, wear more Earth clothing details. In Earth: we wear styles that are timeless and enable us to be easygoing.

If your goal is **to improve more**, wear more Metal clothing details. In Metal: we wear styles whose superior quality and optimal design inspire self-improvement.

Choose only those that you love, the ones that resonate with you.

FASHION FENG SHUI FOR MEN

Creating a deeper and more intense life requires the strength of The Philosopher.

Here's how to dress:

Expression:	Artistic, unstructured, original, reflective.
Looks:	Avant-garde, flowing, unique, unusual.
Hues:	Black, charcoal, navy, sapphire, cobalt.
Fabrics:	Interlock jersey, Jacquard wool mixes, unnatural fibers.
Style:	Expression of a certain nonchalance.
Signature pieces:	Unstructured, loose-fitting, ethnic prints, velvet, moccasins.

Raising your self-confidence to build up your competitor profile requires the strength of The Pioneer.

Here's how to dress:

Expression:	Casual, sporty, athletic, toned, free in movement, action-based.
Looks:	Healthy, youthful, fresh.
Hues:	Light green, light teal, denim, blue-green.
Fabrics:	Cotton, linen, pure natural fabrics, corduroy, denim.
Style:	Very basic, uncomplicated, sporty, leisurely, straight lines.
Signature pieces:	Botanical prints, straight silhouettes, flip-flops, sneakers.

Raising your self-confidence in touching other people's lives requires the strength of The Pleasure Seeker.

Here's how to dress:

Expression:	Attention seeking, lively, fearless, charming.
Looks:	Rock & roll, out of the ordinary.
Hues:	Hot pink, fuchsia, purple, red.
Fabrics:	Leather, fake fur, Lycra, silk, woolens.
Style:	Striking, daring, showy, obvious.
Signature pieces:	Colored lined jackets, diamond patterns, unusual eye-catching details.

Raising your self-confidence in being nurturing mode requires the strength of The Peacemaker.

Here's how to dress:

Expression:	Traditional, non-conformist, self-accepting, unpretentious.
Looks:	Comfortable in your clothes.
Hues:	Browns, bronze, rust, burnt orange, deep yellow.
Fabrics:	Tweed, nubuck, suede.
Style:	Chinos, combined styles, classic with a modern touch.
Signature pieces:	Double breasted jackets, checked or plaid trousers, blazers.

FASHION FENG SHUI FOR MEN

Raising your self-confidence as someone who is impeccable looking requires the strength of The Perfectionist.

Here's how to dress:

Expression:	Stylish, trend-conscious, standing out, memorable, cultivated.
Looks:	Very sophisticated, orderly with class, elegant.
Hues:	Grey, platinum, light blue, pale green
Fabrics:	Pied de poule, high-quality refined woolens, cashmere, polished textures.
Style:	Chic, elegant touch, sense of status.
Signature pieces:	Dandy style, button-up shirts, Windsor ties, Oxford shirts, single-breasted suiting, Polka dot shirt or ties.

Conclusion

Applying the five elements along with the principle of yin and yang can enrich our lives by creating a harmonious balance in our dressing techniques. Yin and yang are opposites of each other—like light and dark, hot and cold—but they need each other to exist.

There may be times in your life that see the rise of specific goals whose attainment requires the strength of specific elements. Fashion Feng Shui® can guide you through this. It teaches you to make empowering choices when getting dressed, to build more confidence in pursuing your goals and to support you in their actual achievement.

This approach to getting dressed allows us to recognize all aspects of ourselves: mind, body and spirit. It allows the five elements to become present around us to interact in perfect harmony and balance. Each element feeds the other. Highlighting your intrinsic qualities, both essential and physical, helps determine which changes you may need to make to better correspond with your elemental archetype. Any changes will have an effect on your everyday balance and the natural you. Breaking free of habits that do not correspond to your authentic self helps you focus on your goal and puts you in touch with your dreams and even unimagined aspirations.

If you have taken time to read through to here, you now know about the person-focused style system known as Fashion Feng Shui®. If you have taken steps to begin incorporating this innovative technique to men's dressing, you should start to reap the benefits in the coming weeks and months. Whether you want to dress in a relaxed, nonchalant style or to the nines in the very best couture, always remember the elemental styles you feel right in. Regardless of your intention: Be true to your essence and go for it.

'Bring fulfillment and prosperity to every aspect of your life'

About the Author

Geraldine Wijsbeek, FFIPI, FFSM, WYEF

Geraldine is an FFS Master Facilitator, an accredited trainer in image and style, a Work Your Element Facilitator and a fellow of The Federation of Image Consultants in London. She has been on the board of the Federation of Image Professionals International (FIPI) as international director and as president, and currently serves as accreditation director. Living in ten different countries over the course of 30+ years has opened Geraldine's knowledge and awareness of colors and of the different cultures of people and their styles of dressing. She has, through experiencing these treasured memories, cultivated an open mindset and become very knowledgeable of the characteristics and aspirations of people.

Fashion Feng Shui® has given her the tools to work with men, women and children by helping them discover their innate elemental energies and teaching them to use this knowledge to achieve the ultimate in their lives. Helping others is truly her passion. Geraldine has studied Chinese physiognomy, an ancient wisdom from China, analyzing important aspects of personality and character. It is based on the principles of traditional Chinese medicine.

She is a passionate teacher, and Geraldine works with color in an innovative way. Styling her clients through Fashion Feng Shui® enables her to determine their inner wellbeing, and her goals are to show them their shining self. She is a people's person and will do her utmost to get a satisfying result which will last a lifetime.

About Fashion Feng Shui®

Create Closet Harmony, Live Your Best Life™

Fashion Feng Shui® stands out from other image practices because it looks at us as whole people. Our clothing choices are as individual as our fingerprints, and our clothing is our most intimate environment. By combining mind, body and soul, Fashion Feng Shui® empowers us to find our unique style so we have confidence in wearing whatever works for us. Fashion Feng Shui® evolves with us as we practice it, so our appearance, desires and lifestyle will always be harmoniously balanced through our closet choices.

In addition to our annual online Facilitator Certification Training Course, we have offerings for individual personal enrichment in the form of the Transform Your Look & Life™ Workshop and the Dress for Your Dreams™ e-course. For those in the corporate market, the most recent addition to our repertoire is the much-praised Work Your Element™ Business Seminar, which adapts Fashion Feng Shui® principles for professionals who consult in a business setting.

Two levels of certification

Fashion Feng Shui® Facilitators (FFSF) are individuals who have successfully completed our 15-week Facilitator Certification Training Course (FCT). They have been awarded the annually renewable rights to offer Fashion Feng Shui® consultations and seminars to clients. Fashion Feng Shui® Facilitators are designated by the professional credentials of "FFSF" after their names. To find a Fashion Feng Shui® Facilitator near you, please visit fashionfengshui.com.

Fashion Feng Shui® Master Facilitators (FFSM) are highly-qualified licensed Fashion Feng Shui® Facilitators who have been awarded the annually renewable rights to offer Fashion Feng Shui® consultations and seminars to clients as well as to professionally train and certify new

Fashion Feng Shui® Facilitators. Fashion Feng Shui® Master Facilitators are designated by the professional credentials of "FFSM" after their names.

Virtual course offerings

Dress for Your Dreams™
This brilliant e-course shows you how to dress for your dreams—step by step, using a mixture of explanation, photos and video. Delivered daily to your inbox in 12 simple stages, it gives you the time and the guidance to implement and see the results for yourself.

Visit dressforyourdreams.com to sign up.

Transform Your Look & Life™ Workshop
Are your clothes speaking your truth? Does every garment express your true magnificence—physically, mentally and spiritually? Does your attire affirm your desires so that you will naturally attract them into your life? On this five-week journey of self-discovery, you learn how to make conscious clothing choices that fulfill your spirit, flatter your appearance, function for your lifestyle and fortify you to attract your desires. Visit fashionfengshui.com to see our schedule of upcoming sessions.

Facilitator Certification Training Course
Innovate or expand your consulting business by joining our international network of Fashion Feng Shui® Facilitators. Discover how our five-element theory provides harmony and balance in our clothing, and how it can help your clients make clothing choices that embrace their mind, body and soul. Over the course of 15 weeks, you learn to select colors, patterns, textures, fabrics and style lines that reflect your clients' authentic selves and help them get what they want.

Visit fashionfengshui.com to see our schedule of upcoming sessions.

Work Your Element™ Business Seminar

Work Your Element™ takes the principles of Fashion Feng Shui® to the workplace, applying our five-element theory to businesses and corporate situations. Understanding and utilizing the positive energy of the elements can enhance business relationships, create productive flow, increase retention of good people, enable them to excel as individuals and teams, and utilize their skill base in work environments.

Visit workyourelement.com for more information.

Contact
Andrew Maggiore, Director
Fashion Feng Shui International
13 Wheeling Avenue
Woburn, MA 01801
USA

+1 781.718.2008
andrew@fashionfengshui.com
www.fashionfengshui.com

For information on our offerings, please contact info@fashionfenghsui.com or call Andrew. You can also find us on Facebook, Twitter and Instagram.

Printed in Great Britain
by Amazon